71720
Avoiding Gridlock

Michelle Lomberg
ATOS B.L: 8.2
ATOS Points: 2   UG

AVOIDING GRIDLOCK

UNDERSTANDING GLOBAL ISSUES

Published by Smart Apple Media
1980 Lookout Drive
North Mankato, Minnesota 56003
USA

This book is based on *Avoiding Gridlock: The Role of Public Transport*
Copyright ©1997 Understanding Global Issues Ltd., Cheltenham, England.

Library of Congress Cataloging-in-Publication Data

Lomberg, Michelle.
  Avoiding gridlock / Michelle Lomberg.
    p. cm. -- (Understanding global issues)
Summary: Explores problems related to dependence on cars; looks at ways
of reducing that dependence, including city planning and mass transit;
and discusses how cities around the world are addressing gridlock,
pollution, and other transportation problems.
Includes bibliographical references and index.
  ISBN 1-58340-357-4 (alk. paper)
  1. Urban transportation--Case studies. 2. Traffic congestion--Case
studies. 3. City planning--Case studies. [1. Urban transportation. 2.
Transportation. 3. Traffic congestion. 4. City planning.] I. Title. II.
Series.
  HE305.L66 2003
  388.4--dc21

                                        2003000107

Printed in Malaysia
2 4 6 8 9 7 5 3 1

EDITOR Tina Schwartzenberger **COPY EDITOR** Janice Redlin
TEXT ADAPTATION Michelle Lomberg **DESIGNER** Terry Paulhus
LAYOUT Bryan Pezzi **PHOTO RESEARCHER** Peggy Chan
SERIES EDITOR Jennifer Nault **CREATIVE COMPANY EDITOR** Jill Weingartz

Contents

NEXT RIG

Introduction

The American love affair with the automobile goes back to the beginning of the 20th century. In 1900, more than 2,300 automobiles were registered in New York City, Boston, and Chicago. By 1910, there were about 500,000 automobiles registered in the United States. Between 1904 and 1908, at least 240 automobile manufacturing companies were established in the U.S. People looked to "horseless carriages" to reduce the noise and manure created by horse-drawn vehicles. Some even believed that car trips were good for their health. However, people also recognized that cars created their own noise and pollution, endangered drivers and pedestrians, and created road **congestion**.

Today, traffic and air pollution are out of control in many cities worldwide. In the U.S., there are more than 200 million vehicles registered. The average family takes 10 car trips each day. Despite these statistics, people are beginning to realize the urgent need to become less dependent on their cars. Whereas cars once meant freedom and **mobility**, today

In total, Americans drive more than 2.7 trillion miles (4.3 trillion km) per year.

they are increasingly associated with gridlock, pollution, and unhealthy, **sedentary** lifestyles. Excessive use of cars is not only damaging the physical environment, but also the general quality of life. **Ozone** created by car exhaust causes dangerous smog and pollution.

The average American family takes 10 car trips a day.

Roads ruin landscapes and neighborhoods. Drivers miss out on the physical and social benefits of walking, cycling, or taking public transit. Increasingly, driver stress and frustration result in incidents of road rage. Car accidents are the leading cause of death for young people ages 1 to 24.

There are additional, indirect problems created by dependence on cars. Mining or extracting metal and oil for building and running cars damages the environment. Underground storage tanks at gas stations can leak, contaminating soil and groundwater. Rain can wash oil, gasoline, antifreeze, and other pollutants into lakes, rivers, and streams. This poisoned water endangers people and wildlife.

Despite their disadvantages, cars offer speed, mobility, and status. They allow people to visit places that are otherwise hard to reach. Car drivers can easily transport groceries, sports equipment, and other goods. It will not be easy to persuade people to give up the convenience of their own cars unless cars become too expensive, or there is a good alternative. Fortunately, many options exist. People can travel on foot or by bicycle. In most towns and cities, they can take public transit. Greater public awareness of environmental issues is also helping people make responsible transportation choices.

THE ROLE OF THE TRANSPORTATION INDUSTRY

The transportation industry is the world's largest industry. This industry includes manufacturing and distributing vehicles, producing and distributing fuel, and providing transportation services. Historically, efficient methods of transportation have been linked to economic wealth and military power. Transportation provides access to natural resources and promotes trade, allowing nations to accumulate wealth and power.

Living with Transport

Gridlock refers to traffic jams that occur when traffic on north–south roads meets up with traffic on east–west roads, causing all vehicles to come to a halt. True gridlock rarely happens because of measures such as timed traffic lights and overpasses that aim to prevent traffic congestion. The term more often refers to traffic congestion in general.

Engineers and scientists have studied traffic jams to find out what causes them and how to prevent them. Researchers have compared the flow of traffic to molecules in a chemical reaction or to data on the Internet. Such comparisons have led to surprising conclusions. Some researchers believe that traffic jams happen spontaneously and therefore cannot be prevented or predicted. Others have proposed that adding more roads to an existing network of roadways only makes traffic congestion worse, not better. Adding more roads simply makes room for more cars.

Such findings do not help the millions of drivers who spend hours stuck in traffic. The amount of time Americans spend driving to work increased

Motor vehicles in the United States consume about 160 billion gallons (610 billion L) of fuel every year, an average of 730 gallons (2,760 L) per vehicle.

14 percent between 1990 and 2000. Much **commuting** time is spent at a standstill. In Fairfield County, Connecticut, commuters spend one-fifth of their driving time stuck in traffic. For Los Angeles drivers, who have the worst traffic in the U.S., time spent in slow or stopped traffic adds up to nearly 136 hours—one week—per year.

The cost of gridlock can be calculated in a number of ways. Some researchers look at the cost of lost work hours and wasted fuel to arrive at a dollar value. In 1999, gridlock cost the European Union (EU) $121 billion in wasted time and fuel. Gridlock has other financial impacts. Traffic congestion causes inflation. When commercial trucks are stuck in traffic, the cost of shipping

The amount of time Americans spend driving to work increased 14 percent between 1990 and 2000.

goods increases, resulting in higher prices at the store. Drivers also pay with their health. The stress of driving in heavy traffic can cause high blood pressure and increased heart rates.

American drivers are not the only ones who experience gridlock. In London, England, the average speed of traffic in the central core is less than nine miles (15 km) per hour. Even China, where bicycles have long been the main **mode** of transport, could have as many as 100 million cars by 2015. Some Chinese cities already have some of the worst air pollution in the world.

The economic and personal costs of gridlock are not enough to get drivers off the road. In 2000, about 76 percent of American commuters drove to work alone. Only about five percent took public transit. There is, however, a glimmer of hope for public transportation.

HOW ARE CITIES FIGHTING GRIDLOCK?

Some cities respond to gridlock by improving roads, encouraging transit use, and discouraging solo drivers. Los Angeles, California, has the worst traffic congestion in the United States. Ninety-seven percent of all trips are taken by car. In response, the city has taken measures to discourage lone drivers. Cars with passengers can bypass gridlocked highways by driving in high-occupancy vehicle (HOV) lanes. Solo drivers must pay for this privilege in **toll** lanes such as the 91 Express. Los Angeles has also taken steps to improve its public transportation system by building one subway and three light rail lines.

Washington, D.C., is second only to Los Angeles in traffic congestion. Experts estimate that in 10 years the time it takes to drive to work will double. An organization called Endgridlock.org recommends the city fight gridlock in three ways. First, existing roads and bridges must be improved. Alternate routes must be provided to remove drivers from the most clogged roads. Second, transit must be expanded. More buses are needed to link the suburbs. Additional light and heavy rail transit lines must be built. Third, people must be encouraged to keep their cars off the road. Washington already leads the nation in carpooling and telecommuting. More HOV lanes and more flexible work schedules will continue to support this trend.

Americans took 9.4 billion trips by public transit in 2000, an increase of 3.5 percent since 1999.

Only cheap, convenient alternatives to urban transport will solve the gridlock crisis. Cities across the United States and around the world are trying various methods to reduce car use and are encouraging more sustainable ways of getting around. Combinations of rail, bus, and bicycle systems are being tried. Traffic is being diverted to create pedestrian areas in city centers. Toll roads and parking restrictions are being introduced. Such advances

> ***Only cheap, convenient alternatives to urban transport will solve the gridlock crisis.***

are only possible because of changing public attitudes.

Public transportation will play the most important role in relieving traffic congestion. If public transportation is to succeed in the United States, it must compete with the convenience of the private car. Effective transportation systems must be cheap, convenient, safe, clean, comfortable, and fast. It is important to remember that the purpose of transport is to move people or goods from place to place. Motor vehicles provide an efficient way of achieving this—but there is a limit to what the roads can carry. We have reached the point where more vehicles mean less mobility.

GRIDLOCK AROUND THE WORLD

Gridlock is a worldwide problem. According to Katie Alvord's book, *Divorce Your Car!*, gridlock in Bangkok, Thailand, has turned the city into something resembling an all-hours parking lot. The only break in traffic usually occurs between 2:00 and 4:00 a.m. Kuala Lumpur, Malaysia; Sao Paolo, Brazil; and Mexico City, Mexico, are major cities renowned for their traffic congestion. The average 1996 workday in Holland generated traffic jams at least 1.2 miles (2.0 km) long. British drivers lose 1.5 billion hours each year because of traffic congestion. There does not appear to be any relief in sight. Forecasts indicate worldwide traffic volumes will double by 2020 and double again by 2050.

MODES OF PUBLIC TRANSPORTATION

The American Federal Transit Administration identifies six main modes of public transportation:

Bus—Buses run on fixed routes along existing roads. They are the most common form of mass transit.

Commuter Rail—Commuter rail systems link city centers with surrounding suburbs.

Heavy Rail—These high-capacity passenger trains run on electric rails. Heavy rail systems include subways.

Demand Response—Demand-response services include cars, vans, or small buses, which pick up passengers on request.

Light Rail—These light, electric trains and streetcars are powered by overhead wires. They carry fewer passengers than heavy rail trains.

Vanpool—Vanpools carry passengers directly from their homes to a regular destination. Vanpool vehicles must carry at least seven people.

KEY CONCEPTS

Federal Transit Administration (FTA) This organization is part of the United States Department of Transportation. The FTA works with communities to provide safe and accessible transit systems that benefit the economy and the environment. The FTA does this by providing leadership, technical assistance, and financial resources.

High-occupancy vehicle (HOV) lanes It is common for larger American cities to reserve special lanes on city highways for vehicles carrying two or more people. HOV lanes are meant to encourage carpools. They also provide faster travel for commuter buses and vans. There are more than 2,500 HOV lanes in North America.

Public transit This term is used interchangeably with "public transportation" and "mass transit." Public transit refers to a system of transportation that carries multiple passengers and is available to the public. Public transit is not necessarily publicly funded. Some buses, vans, and demand-response vehicles are privately owned and operated.

Land Use Planning

At its best, land use planning considers the physical, social, and economic aspects of communities and examines the connections between them. Planners analyze issues such as transportation, land use, housing, recreation and open space, community services, natural and cultural resources, population, and economic development. For transportation, the most effective city plans balance the needs of drivers and transit users, pedestrians, and cyclists. The least effective plans

> *Cities that were planned before the automobile naturally fit the needs of pedestrians.*

neglect public transportation, discourage walking and cycling, and create traffic problems.

Cities that were planned before the automobile naturally fit the needs of pedestrians. The centers of older North American cities and most European cities are dense and compact. They can be easily crossed on foot. Shops and workplaces are built close to homes. Homes are more often low-rise apartments or townhouses rather than single-family houses with large yards. Such neighborhoods demonstrate two principles of sustainable city planning: high density and mixed use.

High-density planning enables many people to live in a small area. Multiple family housing units, such as apartments or townhouses, are preferred to single-family houses. Lots are smaller, bringing buildings closer together. High-density cities or neighborhoods can be crossed on foot, reducing the need to drive.

According to the population and land area figures from the 2000 U.S. census, the highest population density in the country is in Union City, New Jersey. The population density of Union City is 51,606 people per square mile (19,732 people per square km). New York City comes in second with 26,404 people per square mile (10,195 people per square km). The lowest population density is in Anchorage, Alaska, with only

The city of Chicago, Illinois, has 100 miles (161 km) of designated bicycle pathways.

NEW URBANISM

New Urbanism is a system of planning inspired by traditional American towns. New Urbanist planning involves a set of principles that can be applied at many levels, from a single building to an entire community. The principles of New Urbanism are summarized below.

1 **Walkability**
   • Most destinations should be within a 10-minute walk of home and work.
   • Streets are designed to be pedestrian friendly. Buildings are close to the street, houses have front porches, garages and parking lots are hidden, streets are lined with trees, and speed limits are low.
   • Pedestrian streets are free of cars except in special cases.

2 **Connectivity**
   • The network of streets is designed to spread out traffic and make walking easier.

3 **Mixed use and diversity**
   • There is a mix of shops, offices, apartments, and homes on the site. The principle of mixed use is applied within neighborhoods, within blocks, and within buildings.
   • A diversity of people—of ages, classes, cultures, and races—also exists.

4 **Mixed housing**
   • A range of housing types, sizes, and prices are built close together.

5 **Quality architecture and urban design**
   • Buildings and public spaces focus on beauty and comfort.

6 **Traditional neighborhood structure**
   • The centers and boundaries of the neighborhood are obvious.
   • There is public space at the center.
   • Neighborhoods contain a range of uses and densities within a 10-minute walk.
   • Highest densities are planned at the town center, growing less dense toward the edge.

7 **Increased density**
   • Buildings, residences, shops, and services are closer together for ease of walking. This enables more efficient use of services and resources and creates a more convenient, enjoyable place to live.

8 **Smart transportation**
   • A network of high-quality trains connects cities, towns, and neighborhoods.
   • Pedestrian-friendly design encourages a greater use of bicycles, rollerblades, scooters, and walking as daily transportation.

9 **Sustainability**
   • The community should avoid damaging the environment.
   • Eco-friendly technologies are used.
   • There is less use of non-renewable fuels.
   • More goods are produced locally.
   • There is more walking and less driving.

10 **Quality of life**
   • Together, the above nine principles help to create a high quality of life and offer spaces that enrich, uplift, and inspire the human spirit.

153 people per square mile (59 people per square km).

Mixed-use planning allows housing, businesses, parks, and services to be built next to one another. For example, a family's apartment might be within blocks of the children's school, the parents' workplaces, and a grocery store. Such planning further decreases the need for cars. Employees can work near their homes, thereby eliminating the daily commute. Two neighborhoods in the Portland, Oregon, area—Orenco Station and Fairview Village—show successful mixed-planning.

THE ABC SYSTEM IN THE NETHERLANDS

The Netherlands has the highest population density in Europe, packing more than 16 million people into 16,033 square miles (41,526 sq km). Transportation is a major concern. The Dutch government has approved a planning system known as the ABC system. ABC aims to make sure that, whenever possible, people can get to the main economic centers using mass transit rather than cars. Locations are classified into three groups:

A. Locations that are easily accessible by public transport (e.g., areas around central railway and bus stations). Shops and offices should be concentrated in this area.
    Commuting by car should be no more than 10 to 20 percent. Parking spaces are limited to 10 per 100 employees.

B. Locations that are easily accessible by both public transport and car (e.g., areas where public transport lines intersect ring roads). Offices may be in this area.
    Commuting by car should be less than 35 percent. Parking spaces are limited to 20 per 100 employees in the largest cities.

C. Locations that are easily accessible by car (e.g., areas along main roads). Land use should be restricted to transport or land-intensive activities, such as agriculture, leisure parks, etc.
    Commuting by car is unrestricted, except that parking spaces are limited to 40 per 100 employees.

The Dutch government cannot force cities to follow the ABC guidelines. However, the public supports the system.

Orenco Station was built near Portland's light rail line. The area includes different types of housing within walking distance of businesses, parks, and a shopping center. Fairview Village offers a mix of houses, rowhouses, and apartments. Housing is built alongside offices, retail space, and services.

Cities and suburbs where gridlock prevails are usually low-density developments with single-use zoning. These factors force residents to use their cars to get to work, run errands, and enjoy leisure time. One example

> *Los Angeles, California, is one example of a car-centered city.*

of car-centered planning is the presence of large "big box" superstores on the outskirts of many cities. Often, such stores cannot be reached except by car. These developments have had a "double whammy" effect. They help to kill off the traditional retail sector in the city, thereby undermining community life. Such superstores greatly increase the use of cars.

Los Angeles, California, is one example of a car-centered city. Originally a small town located around a railway station, Los Angeles developed around the Pacific Electric Railway, the

▨▨ **Almost 70 percent of commuters in Los Angeles drive to work alone. Only 9.5 percent rely on public transportation to get to work.**

most extensive **suburban** rail system in the world. Passenger service was discontinued in the early 1950s in the face of competition from buses and private automobiles. Los Angeles has not only become a symbol of the car-based city, it also has the worst gridlock in the country.

Los Angeles is not alone in devoting a lot of space to cars. The average city allocates one-third of its land to cars, including roads, service stations, and parking lots. Cities have sacrificed "exchange space," areas where citizens can meet on foot, in favor of "mobility space," areas for roads and car parks.

Instead of designing towns and cities to accommodate cars, progressive urban planners look at ways to make neighborhoods more human. After all, quality of life depends on many factors, such as clean air, safety, and pleasant surroundings, not just convenience. Walking along a tree-lined street is a much more positive experience than sitting in a traffic jam.

▨▨▨ **Only seven percent of Los Angeles commuters rely on buses and trains for transportation.**

KEY CONCEPTS

Zoning Zoning is the practice of assigning different uses to different areas of a city. The most common uses are commercial, residential, and industrial. Zoning can dictate that offices be built in the city center, houses in suburbs away from the center, and factories on the outskirts of a city. Zoning also affects the density of buildings within an area. Urban planners and other city officials are responsible for zoning.

Density Population density refers to the number of people within a given area. It is usually measured as the number of people per square mile. Housing density is measured in the number of housing units per acre. A housing unit can be a house, apartment, townhouse, etc.

Sustainability To sustain means to continue. Sustainability refers to how long a certain practice can continue without becoming harmful to people or the environment. Walking, cycling, and taking public transit are considered sustainable transportation options because they use fewer resources than driving and, therefore, do less damage to the environment.

Biography
Robert Moses

Born: December 18, 1888, in New Haven, Connecticut
Died: July 29, 1981
Education: Ph.D. in political science from Columbia University
Legacy: Expanded New York state's park system and built numerous bridges, tunnels, **expressways**, and parkways

Navigate to Long Island History at **www.lihistory.com/7/hs722a.htm** to learn more about Robert Moses. Also, click on **www.nycroads.com/roads/robert-moses** to learn about the Robert Moses Causeway.

People in Focus

Robert Moses was a city and state official whose vision shaped much of New York City, especially Long Island. Although his legacy includes numerous roads, bridges, tunnels, parks, public housing projects, and cultural landmarks, Moses is a controversial figure.

Born in New Haven, Connecticut, in 1888, he grew up in New York City. Moses was well educated, receiving degrees from Yale and Oxford universities. He also earned a Ph.D. in political science from Columbia University. Moses's long career spanned four decades. He was appointed to head the parks commissions of New York and Long Island in 1924. In 1933, he became New York City parks commissioner and head of the Triborough Bridge and Tunnel Authority.

Perhaps Moses's greatest accomplishment was the development of Jones Beach. Jones Beach was a deserted, swampy sand bar that Moses turned into one of the world's finest public beaches. Over his long career, he expanded the state's park system and created beautifully landscaped parkways. Moses was also responsible for the creation of Shea Stadium, Lincoln Center, and the New York Coliseum.

Critics of Robert Moses hold him responsible for New York City's traffic problems. The highways he built to carry people to his parks are now gridlocked commuter roads. Perhaps the strongest criticism of Moses is that he worked against public transit. He is seen as a key contributor to congestion on the Long Island Expressway because he neglected to ensure that mass transit tracks were built on that road. Even worse is the accusation that he had the bridges on his parkways built too low for buses to pass under, denying people without cars access to parks and beaches.

Light and Heavy Rail

Americans took nearly 300 million trips by light rail and more than three billion trips by heavy and commuter rail in 2000. Light rail includes both streetcars and light rail vehicles (LRVs). Streetcars and LRVs run on electricity from overhead lines. In general, streetcar tracks are built on existing roads and run with traffic, while LRVs run on tracks separated from vehicle traffic. Heavy rail refers to larger trains on electric tracks, such as subways and elevated railways. Commuter trains usually have **diesel**-fueled engines and run on standard tracks between communities. These differences, however, are often blurred, as modern streetcars, LRVs, and even subways share more and more similarities.

Many transportation planners see light rail as a nonpolluting answer to mass transit needs. In addition to being emission-free, light rail offers other benefits. Travel by light rail is safe and speedy. LRVs run more frequently than buses and run on tracks separate from vehicle traffic. Streetcar and LRV lines are much cheaper to construct than subways.

More than 160,000 passenger trips are taken each day on London, England's Docklands Light Railway.

Streetcars, also called trolleys or trams, were once common in American cities. The earliest streetcars were pulled by horses or mules. Electric streetcars were introduced in the early 1900s. These streetcars traveled at an average speed of 12 miles (20 km) per hour. They were uncomfortable to ride and awkward to board. Many cities phased out their streetcars long ago as people turned to private cars to get around. Today, some cities have revived their streetcar lines. In some cities, **vintage** streetcars give residents and tourists a taste of urban history. Elsewhere, modern streetcars complement existing transit services.

In Strasbourg, France, the opening of a single streetcar route increased overall use of the transit system. Since 1990, transit use in Strasbourg has increased by 40 percent, while car traffic into the central core area fell by 17 percent.

There are at least 25 LRV systems in the United States, and many plan to expand their service. Modern LRVs are comfortable, efficient, and easy to access. In the most modern trains, low-level boarding and wide doors mean that passengers can simply walk straight into the tram, instead of having to climb up steps. Attractive design, light, airy interiors, and user-friendly route information help to take the stress out of the journey. LRVs typically run at street level, although in some cities, the routes may be partly underground or elevated. Modern light rail vehicles can

---

There are 25 LRV systems in the United States, and many of these have plans to expand their service.

---

be designed for both low-speed, city center operation and high-speed suburban travel.

Heavy rail systems and commuter trains are effective ways to move large numbers of people. Subway lines can carry 40,000 to 50,000 passengers in one hour. Subways are, however, expensive to build. Many subway systems operate at a loss because they are expensive to build and operate, and because they are only heavily used during rush hours. Subways cannot usually be justified for cities with fewer than one million residents.

Subways are expensive because they must be built, at least in part, underground. Two basic construction methods are used for underground lines. In the "cut and cover" method, a deep trench is cut, lined, and then re-covered. For deeper sections, underground tunnels must be bored. River crossings can be handled in two ways.

TAKE THE TRAIN

For short trips between cities, taking the train can be faster and cheaper than driving, or even flying.

The chart below compares the cost and travel time of three trips by train, car, and plane. Travel time includes the time it takes to get to the station or airport and board the train or plane.

TRIP	DISTANCE	TRAIN	CAR	PLANE
San Diego, CA, to Los Angels, CA	130 miles (209 km)	Time 2:45 $13	Time 2:24 $25–$62	Time 2:30 $152–$546
Chicago, IL, to Milwaukee, WI	90 miles (145 km)	Time 1:40 $19	Time 1:50 $18–$45	Time 2:30 $122–$262
New York, NY, to Albany, NY	156 miles (251 km)	Time 2:30 $33	Time 3:12 $32–$78	Time 3:30 $175–$255

River crossings may be bypassed by tunneling or by lowering ready-made sections onto the riverbed. Some subway lines have sections that run on the surface or on elevated tracks. There are about 15 heavy rail subway systems operating in the U.S.

Commuter train systems are designed to move large numbers of people over relatively short distances, usually no more than 100 miles (161 km) in either direction. Typically, they are used by people going to and from work. Commuter train service has grown a great deal in the past decade. Of the 22 commuter rail lines in North America, 12 were built in the last 12 years. The sharp climb in commuter rail's popularity is the result of public awareness of environmental issues, suburban population growth, government emission-control policies, and traffic congestion.

Despite the environmental and human benefits of rail travel, mass transit alone will not solve America's traffic problems. Experience has shown that the introduction of a rail system takes relatively few cars off the road. The problem is that freer streets tend to attract car users again, just as building new roads attracts more traffic.

The Queens subway line in New York City has a total of 42 miles (68 km) of track.

HISTORICAL STREETCARS

There are at least 18 historical streetcar systems operating in the United States, and more have been proposed. In several American cities, vintage streetcars function as moving transit museums. San Francisco, California; Tucson, Arizona; and Seattle, Washington, all use their streetcar lines to capture their cities' histories.

Residents of San Francisco enjoy streetcars so much that they held an annual San Francisco Historic Trolley Festival from 1983 to 1987. This event brought historical streetcars from across America and around the world to Market Street. Today, streetcars are both an attraction and an integral part of the transportation system. The San Francisco Municipal Railway has 17 streetcars in regular service. Many are painted to look like historical streetcars from other cities.

Tucson had electric streetcars from 1906 to 1930. The city revived its historical streetcar line in the mid-1980s with the Old Pueblo Trolley.

The George Benson Waterfront Streetcar line operates along the waterfront in Seattle. Operating since 1982, this streetcar line features streetcars built in 1927. The elegant wood interiors give passengers a sense of bygone days.

KEY CONCEPTS

Subsidization Services such as transportation are subsidized when governments pay for them with money collected through taxes. People who object to the subsidization of mass transit and other services often feel that they are paying for services they may not use personally. Others argue that subsidies enable all citizens to benefit from services that would not otherwise be affordable to most people.

Emissions Emissions are the chemicals released into the atmosphere by burning fuel. Vehicle emissions include carbon dioxide, carbon monoxide, and nitrous oxide. These emissions, called "greenhouse gases," are believed to be responsible for global warming. Several states have instituted policies to reduce greenhouse gas emissions. Light and heavy rail systems, viewed as possible solutions, are important to some of the policies.

The Benefits of Buses

The bus is by far the most popular type of public transportation in the world. More than 75,000 buses covering more than two billion miles (three billion km) per year operate in the United States. In 2000, more than five billion bus trips were taken in the U.S.—far more trips than all other mass transit modes put together.

Bus travel reduces the number of automobiles on the road, improving traffic flow, conserving fuel, and reducing air pollution. Buses cost less to operate and use less fuel to carry a passenger a given distance than most other passenger vehicles. Bus systems are inexpensive to build and maintain. Buses run on existing roads and require an inexpensive **infrastructure** of garages, stops or shelters, and signs. Buses themselves are inexpensive. In less developed countries, bus travel is one of the cheapest forms of motorized transportation. Buses also have a good safety record, especially compared to cars.

Despite their popularity, buses have a bad reputation when compared to light rail

In less developed countries, bus travel is one of the cheapest forms of motorized transportation.

systems. People see buses as less efficient than light rail systems. Environmentalists compare buses that run on diesel fuel with light rail, which runs on electricity. They say diesel fuel causes pollution, even though the electricity that runs the LRV may well be produced by burning coal.

New developments in buses and bus systems mean some buses surpass light rail in both cleanliness and efficiency. New engine and fuel technologies are allowing buses to run cleaner and cheaper. In 1997, Chicago, Illinois, began a pilot program to test three buses running on **hydrogen** fuel cells that emit water vapor.

London, England's double-decker buses have become more than a simple solution to transporting more passengers in a single bus. They are a symbol of London and a convenient means of transportation.

A MODEL BUS SYSTEM IN BRAZIL

Curitiba's world-famous bus system features express busways that fan out from the city center. Curitiba has few traffic jams, despite having Brazil's second-highest number of cars per capita. Although many people own cars in Curitiba, three-quarters of the population relies on the bus to get to and from work.

The transport network is managed by a city authority that lays down operating rules, sets timetables and routes, and monitors performance. The buses themselves are run by private companies, licenced by the city authority. Each company is paid on the basis of distance traveled. It is a simple system that works.

A single bus route in Curitiba may carry as many as 300,000 passengers each day. The system is closely connected with housing developments, shopping, and leisure facilities. Major stops have become **interchanges** where people can shop, get a cup of coffee, or meet their friends. In this way, the bus becomes a natural and enjoyable part of the social life of the city. Curitiba has become a model for bus systems around the world.

The test program was intended to discover how fuel cell buses work in real life situations, to understand the unique needs of a fuel cell bus system, and to promote public acceptance. The buses proved both efficient and popular. Many transit users were so impressed with the hydrogen buses that they would wait longer to ride them rather than boarding diesel buses, making the program a success.

Boise, Idaho, converted its bus fleet to compressed natural gas (CNG) from diesel. CNG burns cleaner than diesel fuel, which reduces air pollution. In Sacramento, California, CNG buses save the city money. Compared with diesel buses, they cost 11 percent less to operate, after accounting for fuel and maintenance costs.

Manufacturers build buses in varying styles and sizes. A bus can carry as few as 8 passengers or as many as 70. Some buses are articulated, meaning they consist of two sections connected by a flexible cover. Double-deck buses are common in European countries and are often used for sightseeing. Over-the-road buses are specially designed for traveling long distances. Underneath the passenger deck of these buses is a baggage compartment. These buses are known as coaches in most English-speaking countries and as motor coaches in North America.

Bus systems are continually evolving, but there is room for improvement. For many people, bus service means long waits, indirect routes, and traffic congestion. Many problems with bus service result from other traffic. Bus transport is most effective when it does not have to compete with other vehicles on the road. In the U.S., highways around urban areas often have HOV lanes shared by buses and private vehicles or busways only used by buses. In fact, when buses do not have to share the road, they can be faster and more cost effective than light rail systems. Improving the use of buses to make them more efficient and economical is part of an initiative called bus rapid

ATTRIBUTES OF A GOOD BUS SYSTEM

The worst bus systems frustrate riders with long waits, crowding, poorly-lit stops, confusing schedules, and high fares. However, such conditions are by no means inevitable. The best bus systems are a pleasure to ride. Qualities of a good bus system include:

- Clean vehicles that are bright, spacious, and comfortable

- Frequent, efficient service

- Simple fare structure with competitive prices

- Clear route and timetable information for passengers

- Sheltered, brightly lit stops with benches

- Speed of movement, using dedicated bus lanes

- Ease of boarding and exiting, using wide entrances without steps

- Availability of tickets and passes

- Use of nonpolluting vehicles

- Security for passengers

transit. Examples of bus rapid transit include measures such as exclusive bus highways, HOV lanes, and improved bus service.

In a 2001 report, the United States General Accounting Office (GAO) compared bus rapid transit and light rail systems in several American cities. The report compared the operating costs of bus rapid transit to light rail systems and found mixed results. In general, bus systems showed higher operating speeds and had lower operating costs than light rail lines. However, the operating costs on a per trip basis did not show a pattern. On average, the capital costs for busways, HOV

Bus transport is most effective when it does not have to compete with other vehicles on the road.

lanes, and arterial streets to operate bus rapid transit are cheaper than the capital costs to operate light rail systems. The capital costs for bus rapid transit averaged slightly more than $23.2 million, compared to $34.8 million for light rail.

The image of the old-fashioned bus spewing black smoke and lumbering awkwardly from stop to stop will soon be outdated. Buses are cheap to run, and they can be convenient and environmentally friendly. The National Safety Council also estimates that riding the bus is more than 170 times safer than automobile travel. All of these factors make buses hard to beat.

BUSES AND POLLUTION

Much of the pollution in urban areas comes from diesel and gasoline-driven buses. Clouds of black smoke coming from buses is a familiar sight in many cities around the world. The emissions from both gasoline and diesel buses can be greatly reduced with better engine design and cleaner-burning fuels. Such measures are being encouraged by tough "clean air" legislation in the U.S.

The Los Angeles Transport Authority recently ordered 370 new CNG buses for use on the city's urban routes, increasing their fleet of CNG buses to 1,570. This is believed to be the largest fleet of CNG buses in the world.

Although newer technologies are available, older buses continue to be used. It does not always make economic sense to replace an older bus that is in good working condition.

KEY CONCEPTS

Fuel cell A fuel cell is a kind of battery. Like all batteries, fuel cells use chemical reactions to produce energy. Hydrogen fuel combines with oxygen to produce electricity in a hydrogen fuel cell. The byproducts are water and heat. Unlike a battery, a fuel cell does not run down or need recharging. A fuel cell will run as long as it has fuel. Fuel cells are very expensive, which prevents their widespread use.

Compressed natural gas (CNG) Natural gas is found in Earth's crust. Automobiles can run on natural gas in liquid or compressed form. CNG is safer, cheaper, and easier to produce than liquid natural gas (LNG). CNG vehicles emit much less carbon monoxide than their diesel or gasoline-fueled counterparts. However, CNG, like gasoline, is a nonrenewable fuel. CNG also burns cleaner than diesel, but it offers only a modest reduction of greenhouse gas emissions compared to gasoline.

Bus Rapid Transit Bus rapid transit is an initiative that seeks to improve the use of buses. A variety of technological and street design improvements may be used. These include traffic signal prioritization for buses, exclusive bus lanes, better bus stations or shelters, fewer stops, faster service, and also cleaner, quieter, more attractive vehicles.

Biography
Geoffrey Ballard

Born: 1932 in Niagara Falls, Ontario, Canada
Education: Geological engineering degree from Queen's University in Kingston, Ontario, Canada, and a Ph.D. in geophysics from Washington University in St. Louis, Missouri
Legacy: Designed and built a hydrogen-powered bus

Navigate to a biography of Geoffrey Ballard at **www.world-nuclear.org/ sym/2002/ballardbio.htm**. Also click on General Hydrogen's homepage **http://home.generalhydrogen.com** to learn more about the company Geoffrey Ballard created.

People in Focus

Geoffrey Ballard's goal is to replace the internal combustion engine. With his success in developing and marketing the hydrogen fuel cell, he may someday achieve that goal.

Ballard was born in 1932 in Canada. He was an average student in school, but he went on to study geological engineering and graduated in 1956. After a job with an oil company that took him from the Rocky Mountains to the Persian Gulf, he went back to school. Ballard earned a Ph.D. in geophysics from Washington University in St. Louis, Missouri.

With his new credentials, Ballard went to work as a civilian scientist for the U.S. Army. During the oil shortage of the 1970s, he was asked to research alternative energy sources. Ballard resigned from the position when he felt Congress was not taking his research seriously. He returned to Canada to pursue his own research interest—fuel cells. He founded a company called Ballard Power Systems, which produces vehicles and fuel cells for buses and cars such as the Ford Th!nk. Ballard retired in 1997 and launched a new company, General Hydrogen Corporation, in 1999. The purpose of this new company is to ensure that hydrogen is available to fuel a new generation of vehicles.

Ballard's achievements have earned him much praise. *Time* magazine named him a "Hero of the Planet." He has been awarded numerous honorary degrees. He received the World Technology Award in Energy in 1999 and received the Göteborg International Environmental Prize in Sweden in 2000. He was also made a member of the Order of Canada, the highest honor a Canadian citizen can receive.

Mapping the World's Roads

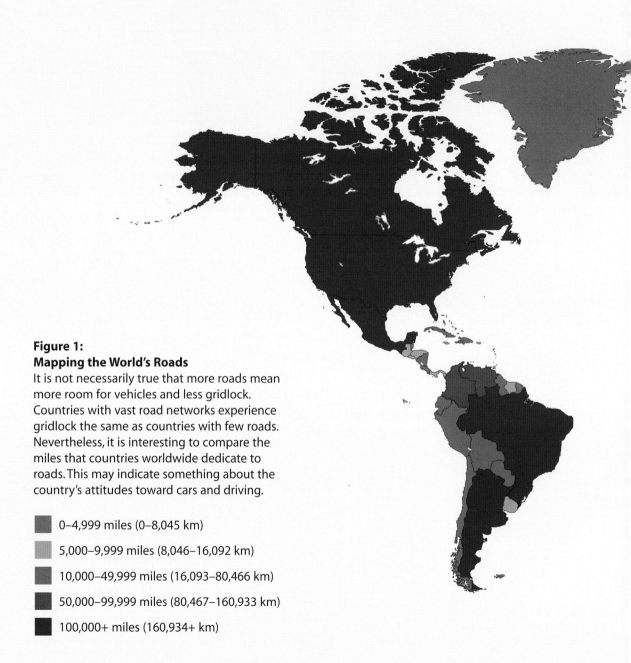

Figure 1:
Mapping the World's Roads
It is not necessarily true that more roads mean more room for vehicles and less gridlock. Countries with vast road networks experience gridlock the same as countries with few roads. Nevertheless, it is interesting to compare the miles that countries worldwide dedicate to roads. This may indicate something about the country's attitudes toward cars and driving.

- 0–4,999 miles (0–8,045 km)
- 5,000–9,999 miles (8,046–16,092 km)
- 10,000–49,999 miles (16,093–80,466 km)
- 50,000–99,999 miles (80,467–160,933 km)
- 100,000+ miles (160,934+ km)

Scale 1:133,056,000

Charting Public Transit Use

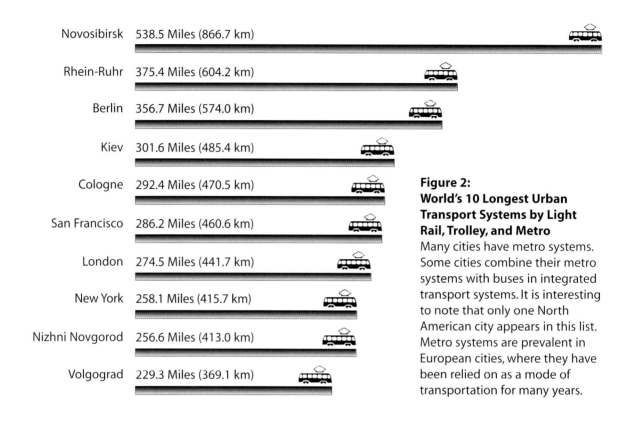

Novosibirsk	538.5 Miles (866.7 km)
Rhein-Ruhr	375.4 Miles (604.2 km)
Berlin	356.7 Miles (574.0 km)
Kiev	301.6 Miles (485.4 km)
Cologne	292.4 Miles (470.5 km)
San Francisco	286.2 Miles (460.6 km)
London	274.5 Miles (441.7 km)
New York	258.1 Miles (415.7 km)
Nizhni Novgorod	256.6 Miles (413.0 km)
Volgograd	229.3 Miles (369.1 km)

Figure 2:
World's 10 Longest Urban Transport Systems by Light Rail, Trolley, and Metro
Many cities have metro systems. Some cities combine their metro systems with buses in integrated transport systems. It is interesting to note that only one North American city appears in this list. Metro systems are prevalent in European cities, where they have been relied on as a mode of transportation for many years.

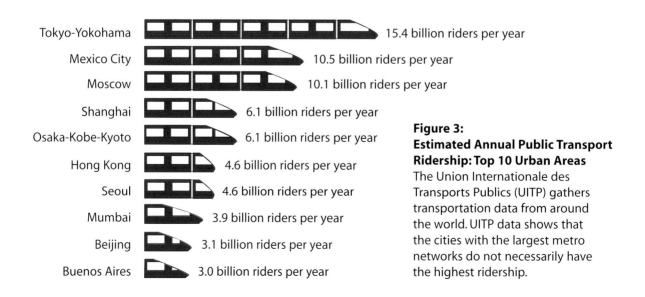

Tokyo-Yokohama	15.4 billion riders per year
Mexico City	10.5 billion riders per year
Moscow	10.1 billion riders per year
Shanghai	6.1 billion riders per year
Osaka-Kobe-Kyoto	6.1 billion riders per year
Hong Kong	4.6 billion riders per year
Seoul	4.6 billion riders per year
Mumbai	3.9 billion riders per year
Beijing	3.1 billion riders per year
Buenos Aires	3.0 billion riders per year

Figure 3:
Estimated Annual Public Transport Ridership: Top 10 Urban Areas
The Union Internationale des Transports Publics (UITP) gathers transportation data from around the world. UITP data shows that the cities with the largest metro networks do not necessarily have the highest ridership.

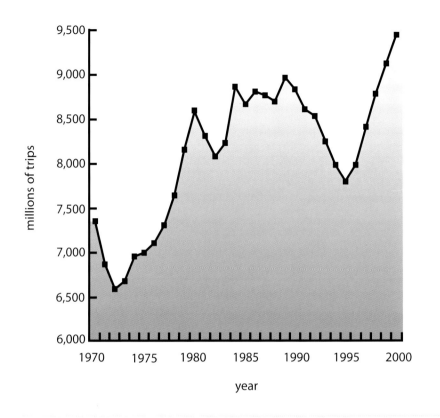

Figure 4:
Long-term Trends in Public Transit Ridership in the United States, 1970–2000
Between 1990 and 1995, public transit use in the United States fell by more than one billion trips. Bus and heavy rail transit experienced large losses in ridership, while light rail transit and demand-response services experienced significant gains. Suburban rail systems increased their passenger levels by five percent in the same period.

Figure 5:
San Francisco Cable Car
San Francisco's world-famous cable cars began operation on September 1, 1873. Today, three tracks traverse 10 miles (16 km) of streets in historic San Francisco.

Curbing the Private Car

To truly avoid gridlock and decrease traffic congestion, attitudes toward cars and driving must change. Governments and private organizations are taking steps to encourage less driving, more carpooling, and car sharing. Cars are expensive

to own and drive. The average American household spends more money on vehicles than on food. Many car-reduction plans use money-based arguments to change drivers' minds.

Cars are expensive. The American Auto Association estimates that it costs $6,400 per year to own and operate a car. That adds up to almost $20 a day. Gasoline is by no means the main expense. In fact, in the U.S., gasoline is cheaper than bottled water. Other costs include repairs,

maintenance, parking, insurance, registration, and tolls.

Drivers also pay with their time. In 1974, author Ivan Illich calculated that the average American spends more than 1,600 hours per year in the car. This includes time spent driving, idling in traffic, and parking. It also includes working to pay for the car and its expenses. Given the increase in traffic congestion over the last 30 years, today's car owners certainly devote even more time to their vehicles.

Nearly 70 percent of British households own at least one car. To curb the use of private transportation, some roads, like this one in Devon, England, have implemented tolls.

Increasingly, drivers are asked to pay for the roads they drive on. One way of doing this is through road pricing, which means that drivers pay to drive on a particular road. There are different types of road pricing, including toll roads, congestion pricing, and high occupancy toll (HOT) lanes.

Toll roads and toll bridges have long been used as a means of paying for highway and bridge improvements. Privately-owned companies often fund road construction by collecting tolls. Tolls may be collected through pre-paid passes, at **toll plazas**, or electronically. The Dulles Greenway is one of the first privately-owned toll roads in the U.S. This 14–mile (23 km) road runs between the Washington Dulles Airport and Leesburg, Virginia.

Congestion pricing is used to reduce rush-hour traffic. In this system, drivers pay higher

---

The American Automobile Association estimates it costs $6,400 per year to own and operate a car.

---

tolls during peak periods. In some cases, congestion pricing only applies to one lane. Drivers can choose to drive for free in heavy traffic, or they can pay to avoid it. Congestion pricing works best for employees with flexible schedules. The Route 91 Express lanes in Orange County, California, are an example of congestion pricing. Depending on the time of day, tolls range between $1.00 and $4.75. The private company that built the lanes collected $20 million in tolls in 1998. In April 2002, the Orange County Transportation Authority (OCTA) purchased the road from the private company. OCTA immediately suggested lowering the tolls and allowing vehicles with three or more occupants to travel for free. OCTA emphasized streamlining the road over profits.

ROAD PRICING WORLDWIDE

Road pricing is probably as old as civilization itself. Tolls are mentioned in ancient Indian texts as early as the fourth century B.C. The English Domesday of 1095 refers to tolls, and London Bridge was a toll bridge in 1286.

Road pricing continues to flourish around the world. France has the world's largest network of toll roads. Toll bridges and tunnels link Scandinavia to mainland Europe. Melbourne and Sydney, Australia, are building underground toll roads to protect aboveground **habitats**. Toll road construction is flourishing from China to the Mediterranean and from Latin America to the Middle East.

In 1991, Trondheim, Norway, became the first city to introduce electronic tolling, charging motorists for every single entry into the city center. Electronic tolling proved successful and has spread to other cities.

In Singapore, drivers are charged heavily for bringing cars into the city. At the same time, Singapore has one of the world's finest public transportation systems, allowing cash-strapped commuters a cheaper travel option.

High-occupancy vehicles (HOVs) travel free of charge in HOT lanes, while other vehicles must pay a fee. On the Katy Freeway in Houston, Texas, the HOV lane is free for cars carrying three or more people. Two-person carpools pay $2.00, and solo drivers are not allowed.

There is some evidence that road pricing, and congestion pricing in particular, reduces traffic congestion. However, this is because more roads are available, not because people are choosing not to drive. In fact, paying to drive well-maintained, high-speed roads might actually encourage more driving. HOT lanes may be more successful in reducing gridlock because they encourage and reward carpools. Road pricing will be most successful when it is combined with an effective system of public transportation. Mass transit should appeal to fee-conscious drivers. Americans living in **transit-intensive** areas save $22 billion each year by using mass transit.

Car sharing is another option that appeals to budget-conscious drivers. Car-sharing networks free drivers from car ownership and offer inexpensive use of a car when one is needed. Car-sharing networks are often nonprofit organizations that offer a fleet of cars and a reservation system. Members of the network reserve a car and access it with an electronic key. Cars are parked around the city, ideally within walking

Carpooling on a 40–mile (64 km) commute saves an estimated $1,300 per year.

distance of most users. Drivers pay by the mile and/or hour. One shared car replaces four to six individually owned cars.

Car sharing has the potential to relieve parking congestion and traffic and to increase transit use. In Switzerland, home to the oldest and most successful car-sharing programs, members reduced their driving by more than 55 percent. A U.S. study shows that car sharers increase their transit use by 20 percent. Forty percent of members gave

up their cars or chose not to buy new cars after joining car-sharing programs. More than 30 car-sharing programs exist or are being planned in American cities. The Flexcar program in Portland, Oregon, founded in January 2000, is the country's oldest.

Reducing the number of cars will help minimize gridlock. Improved public transportation and increasing expenses may help dissuade people from purchasing their own cars.

THE EXTERNAL COSTS OF DRIVING

There are many costs over and above the price of buying a car and keeping it on the road. These costs are borne by drivers and non-drivers alike. The external costs of road transport include:

• Traffic congestion

• Air and noise pollution

• Deaths and injuries from road accidents

• Human health effects of reduced exercise

• Damage to buildings, bridges, and other structures by traffic vibration

• Destruction of wildlife and countryside by road building and traffic

• Social isolation

• Environmental damage caused by oil exploration and the transportation of fuel across sea and land

• Global warming

KEY CONCEPTS

Electronic tolling Tolls are collected electronically using special equipment on cars and at the collection site. Cars are fitted with a transponder that communicates with an antenna at the toll plaza. The driver sets up and pays for an account. The transponder and the toll plaza antenna communicate to debit the driver's account each time the car passes a toll site. If the car has no transponder, or if the driver has no money in his or her account, a video camera records the license plate, and a bill is sent to the driver's home.

Private roads The building and maintenance of roads and bridges has traditionally been a government service. Private companies are increasingly undertaking the creation and upkeep of transportation routes. Governments use tax money to pay for road construction. Private companies may receive government money, but they also look to investors and toll payers for funding.

Nonprofit organization Many car-sharing programs in North America are run by nonprofit organizations. Nonprofit organizations may charge fees and accept donations, but this money goes back into the program. None of the income is given to the organization's members or directors.

Cities Are for People

Walking, cycling, and mass transit do more than relieve traffic congestion. They also enhance the social life of cities. Unfortunately, walking and cycling have become rare in many American cities. In cities built for cars, walking and cycling can be unpleasant, even dangerous. The loss of pedestrians causes businesses to close or relocate to the suburbs. Empty streets become threatening places, further discouraging foot traffic, and inviting crime and vandalism.

Often, walking and cycling are seen as hobbies, not as modes of transportation. Paths and walkways may wind through parks far from workplaces or schools. For those commuting by bicycle or on foot, there is often no choice but to risk their lives in traffic.

There is, however, evidence that attitudes are changing. Some cities are investing in bicycle and walking paths, car-free districts, and traffic-calming measures. Individuals and advocacy groups are fighting for their rights as cyclists and pedestrians. At the same time, they are fighting the battle against gridlock.

Groups such as the League of American Bicyclists and the National Center for Bicycling and Walking lobby for better

In Denmark, walking and cycling are primary modes of transportation. In 1962, the capital, Copenhagen, began transforming from a car-oriented city to a people-friendly one.

CRITICAL MASS

"We aren't blocking traffic—we ARE traffic!" is the rallying cry of Critical Mass, a monthly bicycle ride that takes place worldwide. Its purpose is to assert cyclists' rights to the road. In a typical ride, a group of riders blocks traffic at an intersection. This leaves a lane car-free for a few blocks. Cyclists fill the lane while vehicle traffic waits for them to pass. Critical Mass rides are generally meant to be friendly gatherings of cyclists, but occasionally there are confrontations with drivers and police. The events can attract hundreds of cyclists.

Critical Mass began in San Francisco in 1992. The idea quickly spread around the world. Critical Mass rides now happen worldwide in 200 cities. The name refers to the number, or "mass," of bicycles required to take over a street. The rides are loosely organized. Posters notify cyclists of upcoming events. There is no central organization, leaving local groups to tailor events to fit their communities.

road and path conditions for pedestrians and cyclists. These groups work with smaller local groups to raise awareness of the needs and rights of bicyclists and pedestrians. The targets of their campaigns are often urban planners and public health officials. The groups research the needs of non-drivers; provide information in the form of reports, newsletters, and Web sites; educate drivers, cyclists, and pedestrians about safety; and train other pedestrian and bicycling advocates.

To encourage more walking, advocates suggest continuous sidewalks, separation between streets and sidewalks, year-round

---

For those commuting by bicycle or on foot, there is often no choice but to risk their lives in traffic.

---

sidewalk maintenance, well-marked crosswalks, traffic signals that give pedestrians time to safely cross the street,

and enforcement of traffic laws. The demands of cycling supporters are just as simple. Cyclists need secure parking, safe bicycle routes, and transit vehicles that can carry bicycles. Pedestrians and cyclists receive many benefits from their activities. People who exercise regularly have fewer symptoms of **chronic** illness. They have healthy hearts and strong bones. They suffer less stress and depression. They are more productive at work and are absent less often.

Traffic-calming measures are addressing the main concern for cyclists and pedestrians—safety. Traffic calming means designing streets to slow traffic down. Traffic calming began in the Dutch city of Delft in the 1960s. These residents did not approve of the highways running through their neighborhoods. They responded by creating "living streets." On these streets, cars are only allowed to move at slow speeds. People have **priority**. Traffic-calming measures include speed bumps, narrowing lanes, dead ends, **median** barriers, **traffic circles**, and textured pavement.

Many European cities followed Delft's example in the late 1970s, setting speed limits of 19 miles (30 km) per hour. Traffic-calming measures were applied to intercity highways through small German and Danish towns during the 1980s.

Many cities in the U.S. are listening to pedestrian and cycling advocacy groups, resulting in improved bicycle routes and walkways. Boston, Massachusetts, is a success story for pedestrians and cyclists. Advocacy groups such as WalkBoston and MassBike

GLOBAL CYCLING TRENDS

Twenty-five percent of city trips in Copenhagen, Denmark, are made by bicycle. The total is even higher in the cities of Gronigen and Utrecht in the Netherlands, where bicycles may account for as many as half of all city journeys. These cities have made cycling easy. Bicycle paths criss-cross the cities, and many roads have dedicated bicycle lanes. Cyclists also get a head start at traffic lights.

In contrast, bicycles in China are losing ground. Although there are more than 400 million bicycles in China, cars are becoming the wheels of choice for those who can afford them.

Despite the increasing popularity of automobiles, China averages less than 1 automobile for every 350 people. Bicycling remains the most common method of transportation.

support car-free transportation. A project known as the Big Dig is actually removing a road. In its place, citizens expect to gain 30 acres (12 ha) of parkland and new, pedestrian-friendly streets. They will also regain access to their waterfront, which has been blocked by the expressway since the 1950s.

Colorado cities are also urging people to leave their cars behind. One example is Pearl Street in Boulder, a pedestrian area in the city's downtown. Once lined with cars, the street now pulses with life. Palo Alto, California, actually pays people to ride bicycles. Cycling city workers are paid seven cents per mile (1.6 km) for business trips.

A survey of commuters revealed that while only 5 percent walked or cycled, 13 percent would travel by bicycle or on foot if the facilities existed. Almost three-quarters of those surveyed supported planning for bicycle and pedestrian traffic. As stories of the declining health and fitness of Americans continue to dominate the news, more people may become willing to walk and cycle, especially if the facilities exist.

Urban parks such as this one in Lima, Peru, provide a place for people to gather and enjoy recreational activities.

KEY CONCEPTS

Advocacy groups Advocacy groups are usually nonprofit organizations that promote their particular cause by asking governments to change laws and policies. These groups are typically funded by grants and private donations. Cycling and pedestrian advocates lobby governments to change laws and planning policies.

Lobbying Lobbying is the practice of seeking support from members of the government. Lobbyists use letters, private meetings, rallies, news conferences, and information campaigns to persuade lawmakers to represent their interests. They may also give information or testimony to government committees.

Public health Public health is the branch of medicine dealing with the well-being of a community's health. Public health involves organizing communities to prevent and control disease and educating people about health issues. Walking and cycling can be considered public health issues because it takes a community effort to ensure pedestrian and cyclist safety.

Duties: Makes recommendations for the best way to use land in cities and neighborhoods
Education: A degree in city planning or urban design
Interests: Research, creating maps and models

Navigate to The U.S. Bureau of Labor Statistics at **www.bls.gov/oco/ocos057.htm** for career outlook information on planning and related careers. Also click on **www.planning.org** to learn about the American Planning Association.

Careers in Focus

Urban planners develop long- and short-term plans for how land will be used in a city or neighborhood. They recommend locations for housing, schools, businesses, and parks. Urban planners may help plan roads and transportation systems to solve or prevent traffic problems. Planners may also make suggestions for protecting environmentally sensitive areas, such as wetlands, rivers, or forests. They are involved in every aspect of city life, from concert halls to sewers.

Planners must keep up with current economic and legal issues about zoning codes, building codes, and environmental regulations. They must ensure proposed facilities will meet a community's needs both in the present, and as demands change over time.

Most planners spend much of their time in the office. They write reports and prepare maps and models on a computer. Planners must be comfortable using a computer, as they use computer databases, spreadsheets, and computerized maps.

Planners may also research the history, ecology, and population of an area. Planners meet with city leaders, community members, and various experts. Often, planners visit the sites they are working on to observe the area's features. They also take note of how people interact with a particular site.

In the United States, planners must be certified by the American Institute of Certified Planners (AICP). In order to become certified, candidates must pass an AICP exam. To be eligible to take the exam, planners must have a combination of educational qualifications and work experience. Candidates with a Master's degree must have two years of experience. Those with a Bachelor's degree need three years of experience. People who do not have a college degree must have worked as planners for eight years.

Integrated Transport

Integrated transport is the coordination of services between two or more transportation modes. Coordination must include schedules, fares, stations, and information. Transportation integration is difficult to achieve. It can be especially difficult because in some cities a variety of private and public operators control the transit system.

Many transit journeys involve more than one mode of transport. Switching between modes can be inconvenient, time consuming, and uncomfortable. Where this is the case, people naturally prefer to travel by car. Integrated transportation systems must consider users' comfort and convenience. Conditions at train, bus, and light rail stations have to be comfortable. They should be attractively designed, with places to sit, shop, and buy food. Interchanges between rail, bus, air, and car-based systems should be seamless and easy to use.

Commuter train passengers could gain from integrated

The province of Ontario, Canada, has an integrated transit system that incorporates rail and bus service. Grand River Transit operates 41 routes throughout three cities and one village.

transportation. Ideally, train stations should be a short walk or bus ride from the commuters' homes. The bus should stop at the train station. Clear, visible signs tell passengers where they need to go, and signage on the

Integrated transportation systems must consider users' comfort and convenience.

platform shows which train is arriving and when. Ideally, commuters would not have to wait more than a few minutes for the train, and conditions would be just as good at the other end of the journey. Signs direct

passengers to the bus or light rail stop, and the bus or LRV arrives within minutes. The final bus or light rail ride should be short and direct. For all this, commuters should pay one simple fare.

Bus and light rail riders, who spend about one-fifth of their travel time waiting at stops, can also benefit from transit integration. Coordinated schedules could reduce their waiting time. Stops should display easy-to-read timetables. New technology can provide electronic displays, which show passengers when the next vehicle is due to arrive and where it is going. Satellites can pinpoint the exact position of a bus along its route and estimate the time needed to travel to the next stop.

EUROPEAN MODELS

Americans traveling in Europe are often impressed at the ease with which they can pass from airport to train to bus to ferry. Many parts of Europe feature seamless integration of transportation modes.

In Vienna, Austria, a single ticket enables passengers to travel by any mode of transport that is most convenient. It is easy to change from one mode of transportation to another. The U-Bahn, a subway system with various cross-city routes, is easily accessed from the commuter rail, bus, and light rail systems. This type of fully integrated system is common to many European cities. A dense network of rail and bus lines connects Frankfurt, Germany, with surrounding towns. The city is also linked to the main routes of other industrial centers. In the Netherlands, a similar system connects the country's most populous cities.

This information has long been provided for train systems, but is now becoming available for bus systems, too.

Transportation integration also has much to offer the cyclist. Cycling can be integrated with all modes of public transit. Bicycle racks on buses enable cyclists to travel longer distances and avoid unsafe routes. Further

Washington, D.C.'s fleet of 1,450 buses is equipped to carry up to two bicycles per bus.

integration measures would allow commuters to take their bicycles on trains and LRVs. Bicycle stations with lock-ups, showers, and change rooms would greatly encourage cycling.

There is also room for pedestrian integration into the transportation system. Pedestrians connecting with transit often face obstacles. Strangely, many bus stops are not accessible by sidewalks. Access to rail transit often features awkward stairs and

intimidating, poorly lit spaces. Shelters can be poorly placed, exposing commuters to bad weather. Benches, if they are present, are sometimes too dirty or broken to sit on. Information is also a problem. Signage is often hard to see or missing. The commuter has no way of knowing if a bus is about to arrive or has just left. Again, satellite technology can be used to provide instantaneous information. Proper lighting and security cameras can help

pedestrians feel safe as they enter and leave transit stops.

Integrated transportation requires effort and resources from governments, planners, and passengers. The federal government of the United States takes integrated transport seriously. Congress passed TEA-21, the Transportation Equity Act for the 21st Century in 1998. The act provides funding for current programs and new initiatives that will improve transportation in the United States. Communities receive grants for transportation **enhancements**, which could take the form of bicycle and pedestrian pathways. TEA-21 allocated $225 million for the planning and development of high-speed rail systems between 1997 and 2001. Individuals are also given more reasons to use mass transit. Workers can now receive $100 per month in transit benefits paid by their employer.

Everybody benefits when using public transportation is made easier. Fewer cars clog the roads, making travel easier for those who must drive. Reduced pollution helps the environment. Walking and cycling improves the health and well-being of individuals. Communities benefit from public spaces that are safe and well maintained. The social life of cities thrives as citizens come together on pedestrian streets, parks, and pathways.

PORTLAND, OREGON

Transportation experts generally agree that Portland, Oregon, is the United States' best city for transportation. It serves as a model for cities across North America.

For pedestrians, Portland offers a walkable downtown and several walkable regional centers. The city has an active walking advocacy group.

Cyclists enjoy well-marked bicycle lanes and bicycle racks on buses. There are bicycle stations offering secure parking, showers, and change rooms. All new and renovated buildings must have bicycle racks. There is even a free bicycle program.

Transit users can get around on the city's efficient and extensive bus and light rail systems. Downtown Portland and its regional centers are built around transit stops. Transportation planning is central to all new developments.

Statistics for the Portland area show only small changes in transportation patterns over the last decade. Nevertheless, they are changes in the right direction.

Portland, Oregon, offers both modern streetcars and a vintage trolley system.

DRIVE ALONE (%)		CARPOOL (%)		TRANSIT (%)		OTHER (%)	
1990	*2000*	*1990*	*2000*	*1990*	*2000*	*1990*	*2000*
73.8	73.1	12.7	12.1	4.8	5.7	8.7	9.1

An integrated transportation system in Chicago, Illinois, allows passengers to reach the O'Hare airport by commuter train, shuttle bus, taxi, or private car.

MOSCOW METRO

With more than 13 million people and 2 million cars in Moscow, Russia, there is increasing cause for concern regarding traffic congestion. Though the number of vehicles within the city increased by more than 250 percent between 1991 and 1998, the main mode of transportation is still the Metro.

As one of the largest urban centers in Europe, Moscow has one of the most efficient subway systems in the world. The Metro covers about 160 miles (256 km) of track and transports about eight million people each day. The world's largest subway, the Metro, opened in 1935. Its 160 stations resemble palace interiors with stained glass windows, chandeliers, marble panels, paintings, and statues. Trains leave the station every 50 seconds.

While the Metro is the fastest, cheapest way to travel around Moscow, buses, trams, and trolleys also operate throughout the city. These systems are often crowded and more complicated than the Metro line. Areas in central Moscow, such as the Kremlin and the Bolshoi Theater, are best traveled by foot.

Moscow is Russia's main transportation center. Elaborate highways and railways connect the city to every part of the country.

Civil Engineer

Duties: Designs and supervises the construction of roads, bridges, and other construction projects
Education: Bachelor's degree in civil engineering
Interests: Math, physics

Navigate to the Occupational Outlook Handbook at **www.bls.gov/oco/ocos030.htm** for more information about civil engineering and related careers. Or click on **www.asce.org** for information about the American Society of Civil Engineers.

Careers in Focus

Civil engineers are responsible for designing and supervising major construction projects. Like all engineers, they use math and science to solve problems. Examples of civil engineering projects include roads, buildings, airports, dams, tunnels, and bridges. Within civil engineering, there are several specialties. These include water resources, construction, environment, and transportation.

Many civil engineers have supervisory or administrative positions. They may work as supervisors on construction sites, designers, construction workers, researchers, or teachers.

Civil engineers usually work near major centers. They often work on-site. Some engineering jobs offer the opportunity to work in foreign countries. Two international examples of civil engineering projects are the high-speed rail systems in Japan and Europe and the Chunnel, an underground tunnel that carries high-speed trains between France and England beneath the English Channel.

The outlook for civil engineers specializing in transportation is positive. More engineers will be needed as the demand for high-capacity, environmentally friendly transportation grows.

Almost all engineering jobs require a Bachelor's degree. To be admitted to engineering school, students generally require high marks in advanced mathematics and science, as well as courses in English, social studies, and computers. Bachelor's degree programs typically take four or five years to complete.

Engineers require a licence to work. To obtain a licence, they must have an engineering degree and four years of related work experience. They must also pass a state examination.

Time Line of Events

1832

The first streetcar in the United States, pulled by horses, begins service in New York City.

1885

One of the first practical bicycle designs, the Rover safety bicycle, is invented in Great Britain.

1897

Boston, Massachusetts, is the site of the first subway system in the United States.

1905

The first gasoline-powered buses in the United States begin service in New York City.

1908

The Ford Motor Company launches the Model T.

1928

U.S. presidential candidate Herbert Hoover promises voters "two cars in every garage."

1936

The U.S. Public Works Administration provides federal funding for mass transit and road building.

1946

American transit use reaches its all-time high of 23.5 billion riders.

1962

The House Rules committee rejects U.S. President Kennedy's request for $500 million to assist mass transit.

1964

U.S. President Johnson signs the Urban Mass Transportation Act, which provides $375 million for mass transit.

1964

Japan launches the world's first high-speed train, the Bullet Train. It is capable of speeds of 124 miles (200 km) per hour.

1965

Consumer activist Ralph Nader publishes *Unsafe at Any Speed*, a book criticizing the auto industry.

1972

Annual mass transit ridership falls to 6.5 billion, the lowest since 1905.

1973

An oil shortage causes oil and gas prices to increase. Transit ridership increases for the first time since World War II.

1976

The Metrorail system in Washington, D.C., begins service.

1977

Ed Passerini builds the first entirely solar-powered car. The car is called Bluebird.

1979

A second oil shortage prompts drivers to buy smaller cars.

1981

France completes its first high-speed rail line linking Paris and Lyon. The trains are capable of traveling 190 miles (300 km) per hour on a specially built track.

1989

The oil tanker *Exxon Valdez* spills 11 million gallons (42 million l) of oil off the Alaskan coast.

Tokyo, Japan's Bullet Train, which transports nearly 10 million people each day, is one of the fastest and most efficient trains in the world.

1990

People with disabilities are given better access to public transportation after the Americans with Disabilities Act becomes law.

1991

Americans fight against Iraq in the Persian Gulf War to prevent Iraq from controlling oil reserves in Kuwait.

1992

The first Critical Mass ride takes place in San Francisco, California.

1998

The Transportation Equity Act for the 21st Century (TEA-21) becomes law.

1999

The first line of the subway system in Tehran, Iran, begins operating.

2000

The government of California plans a network of high-speed trains. This plan will be carried out over the next 20 years.

2003

Honda introduces the Civic Hybrid. This is the first mass-produced vehicle combining a gasoline engine and electric motor to be offered in the United States.

Concept Web

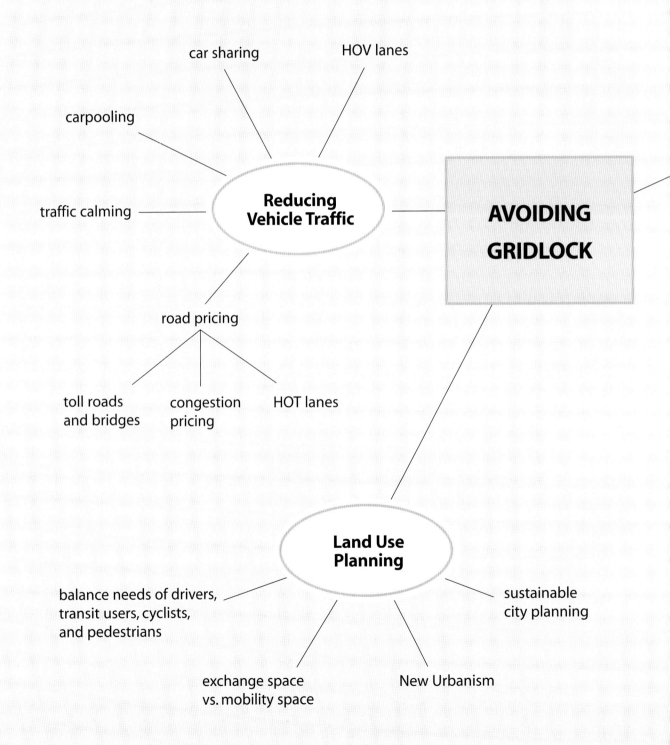

car sharing

HOV lanes

carpooling

traffic calming

Reducing Vehicle Traffic

AVOIDING GRIDLOCK

road pricing

toll roads and bridges

congestion pricing

HOT lanes

Land Use Planning

balance needs of drivers, transit users, cyclists, and pedestrians

sustainable city planning

exchange space vs. mobility space

New Urbanism

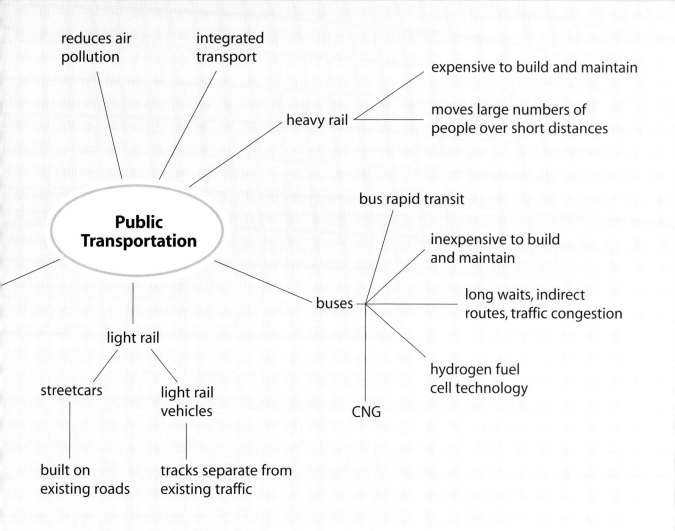

reduces air pollution

integrated transport

heavy rail
- expensive to build and maintain
- moves large numbers of people over short distances

Public Transportation

bus rapid transit

buses
- inexpensive to build and maintain
- long waits, indirect routes, traffic congestion

hydrogen fuel cell technology

CNG

light rail

streetcars
- built on existing roads

light rail vehicles
- tracks separate from existing traffic

MAKE YOUR OWN CONCEPT WEB

A concept web is a useful summary tool. It can also be used to plan your research or help you write an essay or report. To make your own concept web, follow the steps below:

- You will need a large piece of unlined paper and a pencil.
- First, read through your source material, such as *Avoiding Gridlock* in the Understanding Global Issues series.
- Write the main idea, or concept, in large letters in the center of the page.
- On a sheet of lined paper, jot down all words, phrases, or lists that you know are connected with the concept. Try to do this from memory.
- Look at your list. Can you group your words and phrases in certain topics or themes? Connect the different topics with lines to the center, or to other "branches."
- Critique your concept web. Ask questions about the material on your concept web: Does it all make sense? Are all the links shown? Could there be other ways of looking at it? Is anything missing?
- What more do you need to find out? Develop questions for those areas you are still unsure about or where information is missing. Use these questions as a basis for further research.

Quiz

True or False

1. Robert Moses was a public transit advocate.
2. Integrated transportation refers to the rights of minorities to use transit services.
3. One busway in Curitiba, Brazil, can carry 300,000 passengers in one day.
4. Vehicles using hydrogen fuel cells emit only water vapor.
5. Subways are an example of heavy rail transportation.
6. Only American cities experience gridlock.
7. Flying is always the fastest way to travel between two cities.
8. Traffic calming began in the Netherlands.
9. Federal law in the United States forbids private companies from owning roads.
10. Transportation is a public health issue.

Multiple Choice

1. What does HOV stand for?
   a) High Output Velocity
   b) Human Orbiter Vehicle
   c) High Occupancy Vehicle
   d) House Order Vote

2. How often do Critical Mass rides take place?
   a) once a year
   b) once a month
   c) once a week
   d) every two years

3. In Los Angeles, what percentage of trips are taken by car?
   a) 97 percent
   b) 89 percent
   c) 75 percent
   d) 50 percent

4. What is the best way to reduce gridlock?
   a) ban cars
   b) build more roads
   c) raise speed limits
   d) improve public transit

5. Which transportation system is the most expensive to build?
   a) subway
   b) light rail
   c) bus
   d) they all cost about the same

6. Which of the following are principles of New Urbanism?
   a) high-density building
   b) mixed-use development
   c) walkability
   d) all of the above

7. When did road pricing begin?
   a) in the 1960s
   b) in the 1800s
   c) thousands of years ago
   d) in 1998

8. Which transportation mode has the highest ridership?
   a) light rail
   b) bus
   c) heavy rail
   d) vanpool

Answers on page 53

Internet Resources

The following organizations are devoted to public transportation issues and education:

American Public Transit Association
http://www.apta.com

APTA members include public transportation systems and other key players, including financial, construction, and planning organizations. The Web site offers current news about public transportation issues. The site's information center features transit statistics and definitions of public transit terms.

Online TDM Encyclopedia
http://www.vtpi.org/tdm

The Transportation Demand Management (TDM) online encyclopedia contains a wealth of information about transportation issues. Transportation Demand Management refers to strategies that result in more efficient use of transportation resources. Articles on this Web site contain detailed information about topics from road pricing to health and fitness.

Some Web sites stay current longer than others. To find other public transportation Web sites, enter terms such as "gridlock," "transportation," or "carpool" into a search engine.

Further Reading

Alvord, Katie. *Divorce Your Car!* Gabriola Island, BC: New Society Publishers, 2000.

Buday, Grant, ed. *Exact Fare Only: Good, Bad & Ugly Rides on Public Transit.* Vancouver, BC: Anvil Press, 2002.

Derrick, Peter. *Tunneling to the Future: The Story of the Great Subway Expansion That Saved New York.* New York: New York University Press, 2001.

Motavalli, Jim. *Breaking Gridlock.* San Francisco: Sierra Club Books, 2001.

Perl, Anthony. *New Departures: Rethinking Rail Passenger Policy in the Twenty-First Century.* Lexington: University Press of Kentucky, 2002.

Answers

True or False
1. F   2. F   3. T   4. T   5. T   6. F   7. F   8. T   9. F   10. T

Multiple Choice
1. c)   2. b)   3. a)   4. d)   5. a)   6. d)   7. c)   8. b)

Glossary

chronic: ongoing or continuous

commuting: traveling to work or school

congestion: blockage

diesel: a heavy, oily fuel that burns less cleanly than gasoline

enhancements: improvements

expressways: roads on which traffic can travel nonstop at high speed

fares: monies paid to travel on a bus, train etc.

habitats: natural areas where plants and animals live

hydrogen: a chemical element that is part of water

infrastructure: large-scale public systems, services, and facilities

interchanges: the sites where passengers switch from one mode of transportation to another

intimidating: frightening

median: a landscaped border separating lanes of traffic

mobility: the ability to move around

mode: type or kind

ozone: the form of oxygen that absorbs ultraviolet rays in the upper atmosphere, preventing them from reaching Earth's surface

priority: highest importance

sedentary: spending much time seated

suburban: beyond the city center

toll: a fee paid to use a road or bridge

toll plazas: places where tolls are collected

traffic circles: intersections with circular structures around which traffic must pass in the same direction; traffic circles are also called roundabouts

transit-intensive: having a high level of public transit service

vintage: from the past

Index

Photo Credits